Even at This Distance

by Ann Knight & W. P. Kinsella

Pottersfield Press, Lawrencetown Beach,
Nova Scotia, Canada
1994

Canadian Cataloguing in Publication Data
Knight, Ann, 1943-
Even at this distance

Poems.
ISBN 0-919001-89-0

I. Kinsella, W.P.   II Title.

PS 8571.N49E83 1994   C811'.54   C94-9501275-1
PR9199.3.K497E83 1994

Cover painting by Lee Harwood
Published with the assistance of the Canada Council and the
Nova Scotia Department of Education, Cultural Affairs Division

Pottersfield Press
Lawrencetown Beach
R.R. 2 Porters Lake
Nova Scotia
B0J 2S0

Table of Contents

INTRODUCTION

ANN KNIGHT

During Holy Week, 1993, I was reading *Six Days In St. Petersburg*, a collection of "return poems" by the Rev. Alla Renee Bozarth, when I found myself reaching for a pen to scribble companion pieces in her book's white space. I've done that in Robert Hilles' books, too. Rather than condemn my marginalia practice, I prefer to praise the poets who summon the voice within me.

Bill (W. P.) Kinsella's poetic language has always awed me. In *Shoeless Joe*, he writes of clouds lumbering off "like ghosts of buffalo," and my jaw drops. In three words, he captures not only the Iowa sky of today, but of two hundred years ago. So, it obviously isn't important that his poems in this volume are twenty years old, written when he was a student of Robin Skelton at the University of Victoria, and reworked, in some instances, when he studied with Rita Dove at the University of Iowa.

Bill sees with the timeless eye of bards before him. I tend to celebrate particulars: the death of Marian Anderson on Maundy Thursday, 1993; the demise of the monarchy in my lifetime. Ideas fuel my work toward vision, while the image propels Bill's visions toward story. I find this sampler a rather typical display from the balance beam we work upon, day by day.

I dedicate this book to those who find themselves living inside out.

W. P. KINSELLA

Ann English (Knight), a Baptist preacher's daughter I met in a writing class in Iowa in 1976 and married two years later, saw her first poem in print when she was seven. It was, she says, a painfully simple question-and-answer affair about the nature of prayer. She continues writing poetry because she believes in heaven.

I believe in Iowa, in retreating to a warm climate to write, in going to McDonald's for breakfast, if at all possible, and in picking Atlanta pitchers for our fantasy baseball team, the Memo Lunatics (of the Sixties Lezcano Ultimate Baseball Association). Ann believes in confession and dialogue. She enjoys doing both in her poetry. But she can be delightfully silly at times, which is reflected in some of the songs she courted me with. She can be observant, emotional, theological, even mystical. I leave the reader to discover those facets of her Muse.

Whenever I produce a poem anymore, it's shorthand for a story (even a novel) I'm working to find a handle for; I want to nail down a few images I can return to, string together a bit of plot, and listen to the character whose voice I'm going to co-opt for some number of pages. Nearly every poem I'd published before turning to fiction appeared in Ann's and my first collection, *Rainbow Warehouse* (Pottersfield Press, 1989). *Stories* have been putting bread on the table for more than ten years. I'm a pragmatist. Poetry is the motherlode, the discipline good writers mine to become fluent in *another* literary form that the public will *buy*.

Ann tells me that good poems put bread on the table, too. They contain something substantial we can sink our teeth into; or something symbolic, a metaphor we can cohabit. Ann spends a good deal of time praising mentors in her poems, wrapping the moments she's shared with them into a few lines of verse. She likes to rehearse her theological positions on the poetic page—something we try *not* to do in day-to-day life, as we're seldom, if ever, in agreement on things reverential.

Ann's poetry, like her as-yet-unpublished fiction, is lean on description, long on the depiction of an emotional reality, her reality: that there's an existence beyond death that makes it possible for one to be patient with life. Although I'm losing my sense of urgency about getting *every* story out of my head that's in there, I do not share the optimism that suggests we carry on with our work, hereafter. The average person finds it impossible to *believe* the unbelievable unless a linguistic magician performs sleight-of-tongue. To accomplish that in a few lines is the perpetual challenge for the poet.

Reviewer Robert Denerstein recently described *Field of Dreams*, my crowning achievement, as "at once the most preposterous, moving and profoundly significant of recent baseball movies." Ann Knight's poetry may be preposterous and profoundly significant. The nice thing for us, is that it doesn't *have to* put bread on the table.

White Rock, British Columbia
Summer 1993

Monday

LIGHTNING: Honor the waiting, period.
THUNDER: Bare your balmy backs to the rain.

LOVERS

AK

trapped in the memory of a glacier
we are covered by frozen sky
ground into an earth that has forgotten her sun

encircled by chilling words, tomorrow withdraws
her history already burned onto the scarred limbs
of dismembered trees

we have been rolled into eternity,
a singular smooth stone totem of winter, and
after the thaw, we will be found intact

An earlier version of "Lovers" was published in WEE GIANT, v. 4 no. 1, 1981.

IRONS

WPK

I made love five times
in the two days
after I met you,
each time pretending,
each time coming away
glass-empty, your name
ringing in my crystal chest.

I want to write your name
so you'll know how frantic
I feel about you, but
the lead shadow of rejection
presses dark above my head.

I feel like an ant
under a flat-iron. Suppose
you say, no, you can't write
your poems to me?
In the distance a sullen sun
reflects off fields of flat-irons
as far as the eye can see.

DETAINEES

AK

We've been detained at this time

To divide those who say the planet

Is dying, from those who can see

She is living. Only false hopes
        and misspoken dreams must die.

        (Honor the waiting, period.)

We're alive in this place of death.

We bury hope where others bury

Death. The Japanese produce an old

Seed. Planted, it sprouts. We don't
        imagine it can bud.

        (Honor the waiting, period.)

        Then today, one ancient blossom sings
        Of life that hasn't flowered in 2,000 years.

        (Honor the waiting, period.)

VANGY'S MOTHER

WPK

Drunken men with wily faces,
Ragged teeth and blue tattoos,
Follow you home
Flop you down.
We children lie still
As logs,
On half of the saggy bed
You and your lover on the other
Bodies splattering hard
Hitting, hitting

My siblings sleep
Burrowing fox-like
Into the sweaty sheets
As you squeak and groan
And stretch for the ceiling
With your long, pale legs.

Mother!
Though I'm grown now,
When passion momentarily
Blots the horror
That swirls about me,
Small animal sounds
Skitter from my throat,
I smell that creaking room,
Feel your lover's heavy sweat
Upon me.
I turn rigid,
corpse cold,
And loathe you, mother,
For stuffing me
With such memories.

PIT LAMPING

WPK

Pale as camellias
She sits in the sun
Nodding her life away

In night fields
A fawn is snapped
In the golden trap
Of headlights, pierced
By yellowed needles,
Flung in the underbrush
To die slowly

Powdered dreams float
In the haze of her eyes,
Soft as lies,
Until they patter away
Little animals
Frightened by the scream
In her blood.

THE CALL

AK

In the year
the church worship service died for me,
I saw the Lord standing in a crowded streetcar
clutching a ceiling strap.

In the press,
a middle-aged man of low social repute
and behind, a drunken woman grasping a small purse.
The Lord smiled at her.

When the bus stopped, he helped her off
and followed her into a bar that was filled with smoke.
Then said I, "Woe is me. For I am unconcerned. I am
a double talker dwelling in the midst of double-talkers
who have failed to see the King."

Then I heard the voice of the Lord say, "Who shall be
opened to worship and to serve me where I am?"
Then said I, "Here am I
Open me."

An earlier version of this poem, "The Calling of a Modern Isaiah," appears in
the *Ottawa University Literary Supplement* of 1964. AK: I took my first two years
of university at Ottawa, a Baptist college in Kansas. Members of my family
had attended that school including Caramita Gage, who later served as a
missionary in China. I was anticipating a life as a missionary in Africa when I
wrote this poem. Only as I explored the abusive aspects of the colonial mindset
did I abandon my determination to Christianize the world. In its narrowest
sense, I still view myself as an evangelist, the bearer of good tidings.

OPENING DAY

AK

I'm a bona fide scout for the Atlanta Braves, registered with the Commissioner of Baseball. In helping my husband track down outfielder Moonlight Graham, I was mis-identified as J.D. Salinger in the *Minneapolis Star*. I co-founded a writers' group which adopted "The Ballad of Amelia Earhart" as its theme song, and the Memo Lunatics (for which I draft ten fielders a season) are presently leading in the standings of the Sixties Lezcano Ultimate Baseball Association. Friend and fan Bill Swank forced the spring of '93 by suggesting we commence a search for "the real" Memo Luna. All this is celebrated in "Opening Day."

"Batter up!" *¿Donde esta Memo Luna?*
Where is Billy Moon, least heat pitcher
of the '54 Cardinals? (In two-thirds
of an inning, Memo racked up a lifetime
earned run average of twenty-seven.)
They printed his baseball card before
his hour upon the stage: "No major league
experience," it proclaims. Prob'ly better.

Finding him, could parallel J.D.'s search
for Moonlight Graham (whose baseball record
was perfected on a Field of Dreams.)
Memo is the reincarnation of that diurnal
quest, a longing to recall the notes
of a song no one's heard in fifty years:
"Happy landings to you, Amelia Earhart,
farewell, first lady of the air."

"Strike three." Our research concludes quickly. *Luna
esta en Los Mochis* (an industrial seaport town one
unpredictably-scheduled ferry ride across from Baja
to the mainland.) We can make the trip next winter,
collect Memo's signature, smile. No mystery is left
to us. We know. But as spring training ends, I relish
having cared enough to learn where one Mexican
baseball legend lays his head, *this* opening day.

Tuesday

AK: Enter the first habitat of the soul.
WPK: Explore the ice-cream morning.

RESERVATION

WPK

An old woman hobbles
across the tuft prairie,
bent, black-shawled,
her ungainly gait
like a crow's
walking away.

GROOMING

AK

At the end of a cast iron bed, an old black woman
with beautiful hands, the household maid, bends

to put a flower in the hair of her mistress,
a woman with beautiful skin. The servant

doesn't comment on the nakedness of her
mistress, but she pauses to stroke the

unclothed petals of the flower. There is an hour
when women know each other in the direction

of an eye, the choice of attire, or the fire
shooting from the tips of their fingers.

A hush hangs in every womb; unnamed,
it is untamed: the first habitat of the soul.

AK: This poem canonizes common wisdom so that uncommon Wisdom may be
approached. (See also: Jeremiah 1:4-5, Psalm 139, Eccl. 12:7, and Acts 17:27-28.)

POEMS BY SILAS ERMINESKIN*

WPK

TEN BEARS

The sun is shine.

The school smell of varnish.
I look out the window
and the whole Eastern sky
is like a movie screen
and Ten Bears, Chief of the Comanches
rides right through the factories
until he looks in at me
as his war bonnet flops in the breeze.

"What you see out there, Boy?"
my teacher wants to know
and she think I dumb
because I don't tell her.

MY SISTER

My sister is marry a white man.
He not a bad man.
He wears a suit and makes money
but he don't fit in with us.
I take a long time one day
To figure why, and what I see is:
he don't make no laughter
and my sister, since she marry with him,
she don't anymore either.

18

NAMES

Coyote, Ermineskin, Yellowknees,
Standing-by-the-door.
Our people are named
for the first thing they see
when they born.
White-face, Pony, Walk-away,
Redbird, Fire-in-the-draw.
White men make laughter on us,
"Funny names," they say,
but what about theirs?
I'd rather be called what I am
than be Smith, for shoe horses.

OCTOBER MORNING

Frost snap at things
and make white whiskers
on the grass.
Outside the cabin door
the dogs are curled
in their dirt nests
and look like horse collars
thrown on the ground.

'Silas Ermineskin is the narrator of one hundred stories most of which are published in story collections by W. P. Kinsella. Kinsella defends his "appropriation" of Silas' voice, saying, "All my characters' voices are my voice. I'm a writer. It's my job to put myself in other people's shoes. There are no stop signs on the imagination. The saddest thing about the politically-correct movement is that it has no sense of humor. Making readers laugh and cry, even in the same breath, is what good writing is all about." These poems were commissioned by Vancouver bookseller/publisher William Hoffer so that they could be translated into Latin.

QUESTION PERIOD

AK

Parallel journeys,
but intersecting lives.
    I stumble across a woman
    with a book in her mouth, titled,
    My Heart Can Find Its Own Way Home.

The persistence of particular snares
moves me to ask, who cares?
    Can Californians find happiness
    in Western garb? Or does the logic
    of karma hold the key to their bliss?

Gravediggers integrate the common and cosmic:
my meaning is not all there is.
    But what shall we do
    with our love, my love, if it
    doesn't run out of steam?

WEST WINDOW

WPK

Chickadee nuns
in a choke-cherry tree
chatter and scold
like old Cretan women.

DISNEYLAND

WPK

Disneyland is the place to be
when you are in love.
Like love, it is unreal —
a mirage in the morning sun,
shimmering white
like the coats of the attendants
with hippo-mouthed dustpans,
who sweep away
imaginary cigarette butts
in the ice-cream morning.

Wednesday

ETERNITY: That which is visible to the lungs.
POSTERITY: Those who appreciate eternity.

R.S.V.P.

AK

I invite you to the place where
Pen and paper open the silence.

SUMO HAIKU

WPK

Soft on the doyho
A yellow chrysanthemum
Plump as a rikishi

Commissioned by the *Denver Post*; April, 1993.

SPY POEM

WPK

On a moonless night
Poem, black silk billowing,
floats earthward
behind enemy lines.

As the mosquito hum
of the plane grows dim,
Poem buries his parachute

Skulks over silent fields
with a message, a revolver
and a poison pill
next to his heart.

ELUSIVE

AK

how is it the poem escapes me
my frantic exhaustion falling in a heap at its feet
my wounds pressing forward to be licked, before
it rides off into the sunrise in search of darkness

how is it the poem escapes me
when I've asked *too many* questions, lurked
in one-beyond-enough for curiosity's sake, dark alley,
and pretended to licenses I don't even want

how is it the poem escapes me, waking me
in the middle of the night with its cadences, asking me
to come to the table and eat its skeleton; refusing to say
where it has left its flesh, who has drunk its blood or when

the dawn will appear

An earlier version of this poem was published in *PEOPLE WATCHER*, No. 74; January, 1979.

MIDNIGHT MASS

WPK

Once, in a man's December
I stood silent
On an ermine street
Breathing a church's varnish breath,
Seeing music crystals,
Moonbeams, and remembering. . .

Once, in a baseball August
We rode without shirts
On a smiling bus
Blowing bubbles with a hoop
And a jar that dripped down our arms,
Bubbles vanished like spoken words
In the window wind. . .

Little prayers, like bubbles,
Floated out toward heaven
To vanish as prayers and bubbles do.

Snow cried under my shoes,
Cried for all the lost Augusts.

TRIVIA

WPK

Like the kangaroo,
there are no fossils of me
anywhere on earth.

ICE FISHING

WPK

Drawn up
they arch and die,
bruises on the ice,
toy eyes
drying
in the wind.

A SECULAR COLLECT FOR A SACRED MAN

AK

For Robert Kroetsch

In his space, another dedicates
a collection of images to you
(where I am caught putting words down)

Not because we ever said that much
directly, but rather, in the frames
you stopped to see (where

Our lives were buried), you slept
eyes open, and planted seasons
you could slow us down in

(Asked me to imagine myself
full enough to make the binary
stop meaning: pro/found con)

Pristine homebody (your corners meet
cleanly behind the bookshelves where
the floor goes to hide, but you can't.)

Tonight, the spice-ridden refrain of a gourmet
evening approaches, as I pare this silence
with a grace I haven't given you before.

Previously published in Calgary's *BLUE BUFFALO*, v. 1, no. 2; Fall, 1983.

CHOKING ON THE DUST OF GOD

AK

Still on assignment at 3 a.m., I stop
to take food for the road in an all-night coffee shop.
"I'm a writer," I explain to the waitress, "temporarily
suffering from uncontrollable flashes of insight, a
deadline, and this leaky congregation of ballpoint pens."

Asking directions, I get
the usual, "You can't miss it."
But I *have* missed something.
That's why I'm making penance with a man
recovering from an overdose of beer.
"A writer!" (He wants company,
and I'm a woman. To him, that spells opportunity).

He prattles off the things he's read
instructing guys on how to pick up girls.
"Pardon me," (I finally frame
a lie to tell the truth for me),
"My husband's waiting."

A previous version appeared in *THE WITNESS*, v. 64 no.2; Feb., 1981.

.22

WPK

A rifle shot at a quarreling flock
Of sparrows. One dropped, soft as the grass
On which it fell. Close death, a chilling shock.
Still, the boy raced home to show the lifeless mass.

Bright eyes glazed-glass, so hushed, the victim bird,
A bead of blood congealed upon its beak.
One last red-berry chirp all that was heard
Before the bullet burst its body weak.

"Bring it to life," his mother said with pain.
Those four words, a shroud, turned *him* cold and still.
"When you can make it fly and sing again,
Then, you will have earned the right to kill."

WPK: I recycled this snippet of autobiographical material for Ray Kinsella's character in *Shoeless Joe*.

EVEN AT THIS DISTANCE
                                    AK

Inventing John Matthew Kinsella

I've answered your silent knock twice.
You breezed in, suggesting, "I have

something I need a hand with."
My hand would do. And, an ear or two.

I'm *your* intermediary, but
whose intermediary are you?

We're answers in a solution grander than
we are. And, we're aware that we are.

SPECTRE

WPK

Does the spectre
of baldness
haunt you?

Next time
you look
into the mirror,
try to visualize
how you may look
five years from now.

Will you have
as much hair
as you have today;
or, will you look
ten years older
because
you have become balder?

WPK: This is a found poem.
    From an ad for Thomas Scalp Treatment.

DAY IN, DAY OUT

Portions of this poem are found.　　　AK

No record exists of any aboriginal names for the days of the
　　week, although "the direction of the sun" was recognized.
　　Bundles of sticks marked the passage of time.

To accommodate the adoption of the Julian Calendar, 45B.C. was
　　assigned 445 days.

The Mayans put 18,980 days onto one cycle, the famous Calen-
　　dar Round. Aztec gods and children were given calendar-
　　related names, and every fifty-secondth year was eliminated
　　entirely.

The Council of Trent ordered Easter's misalignment corrected. So
　　Pope Gregory XIII declared that Oct. 5, 1582, become Oct. 15,
　　to adjust the vernal equinox. As part of his package, centuries
　　not divisible by 400 (1700, 1800, 1900) lost their leap year day.
　　In Britain, Sept. 3, 1752, became Sept.14, to bring the mon-
　　arch's peoples onboard the Gregorian system.

The twelve months of the French Republican Calendar were
　　renamed: Vintage, Mist, Frost; Snow, Rain, Wind; Seedtime,
　　Blossom, Meadow; Harvest, Heat and Fruits. This calendar
　　weathered from 1792 to 1806. During the revolution, these
　　months had three weeks of ten days each. Rest was allowed on
　　the tenth day.

An International Calendar has been proposed adding a thirteenth
　　month, Sol, between June and July. Every month would begin
　　on a Sunday and end on a Saturday. Your birthday would
　　always fall on the same weekday, and there'd be one "un-
　　named day" each New Years, and a leap day after every
　　fourth June.

A World Calendar, more satisfactory to the business community,
　　proposes four 91-day quarters every year (a 31-day month,
　　followed by two 30's). There'd be an "extra day" following
　　every Dec. 30, and leap days every fourth June 31.

Disclaimer: Due to the dominance of Christian-era practice, present under-
standing of former systems may not reflect their complexity. Tolerance for
others' calendars is assumed to be at its nadir.

A COUNTERBOMB RENGA
THAT NEVER LEFT THE HOUSE

AK

For Peg, who had that extra baby and
put in long hours for Uncle Sam.

> She worked on the *theory* of war
> Erasing estimates, recalculating
> Collecting and evaluating data
> On the wind-tunnel bomb
> Never-to-be, but suddenly
> Dropped on Hiroshima.
>
> She, is my friend Peg, mathematician
> Escape artist, survivor; let's
> X the box beside
>
> **FEMALE** and put another body in a coffin
> Peg did the figuring for; to which none of her
> three daughters could ever conscientiously **OBJECT**

AK: In the summer of 1982, a Hamilton-based poet, Udo Kasemets, inspired by Jonathan Schell's book, *THE FATE OF THE EARTH*, undertook to link Canada's poets as the Concerned Artists Demanding Abolition of Nuclear Arms or, CADANA. That was the summer Bill and I were touring to promote his first novel. I wrote this renga then, according to Udo's complicated instructions, but *Notebook #15* never got out of the house. "There's no time to be wasted. Let's connect," was Udo's parting injunction, just as "Honor the waiting, period," is my opening salvo. If anyone's run into Udo's "wordless chain-charts based on the renga principles and to be presented later in conjunction with the spoken words," please drop me a line to that effect.

Thursday

DAWN: Sleep the sun into your frail assemblage of limbs.
DUSK: Sign-in on the ink between stars.

THANKSGIVING

AK

For Alla Renee

Empress of beehives, shameless Sister,
you sleep the sun into your
frail assemblage of limbs; enter
light, with your eyes closed.

The invisible dawn approaches
from behind your mountain
signing-in on the ink between stars:
Here's tomorrow to do your love upon.

Hide with the flowers. Then
Rise at your appointed hour to
annoint the energy of a name.
For flesh *is* a reluctant medium.

Learn your way around in the
chambers of my heart where
bare hands tell the whole story:
allegiance is the last virtue.

REUNION ONCE REMOVED

AK

I search for my bones.
Did I lay them here?
Has the marker been moved,
Or memory distilled, so
Only God can discover
My path through the stars?

DAY AFTER INAUGURATION '93*

AK

Your rock, Maya. Your tree.
You, behind that podium. Your
all-embracing voice slows me
To the pace of the passing parade.

I'm passing. I'm passing on—
Passing, on blame and shame,
On needless suffering. I'll pass on
Horror, but can't ignore its victims.

I see the hour of our salvation. I've
Learned when to cross your river,
Maya. Follow me. *Follow me*, echoes
A child. *And bring your rock with you.*

And bring your rock with you, I answer.

"Day after Inauguration '93" appeared in *RUACH*, the newsletter of the Episcopal Women's Caucus; Fall 1993.

APODA

WPK

I
And it is said, God created man in his own image.
But what was that image? Was it what God saw
When He looked at His reflection in the night sky?
Or was it what He wanted to see, wished to see?
Was it God, as seen through other eyes?
The eyes, perhaps, of a silken bird as blue as the sky
And so far away from earth that it was known to God alone.

God, it is said, created man in His own image, but
Suppose that image was how God looked to the bird
He had created to fly a lifetime high and free.
High in the purified ice-blue air where freedom
Is loneliness, and loneliness, the price of freedom.

II
And if man was conceived from a bird's-eye-view,
And sane men seldom say they have faced God
And returned, could it be that those who find the
Body of the footless bird, those who cradle the
Feather-light form in their hand, are holding
More of God than those who clutch cross
And crucifix, beads and idols?

Is it possible that generations of men have knelt
With arms raised in praise to a bird, a footless bird
As ephemeral and elusive as God, as hard to find
And hold as God, as hard to believe in as God?
Like silver rings through silver rings, a puzzle
Without a solution; only the uncorrupted can find God,
Yet only those corrupted by life bother to search.
Can it be that God's one perfect creature is for
His eyes alone? Or, is this, too, too gross a vanity?

III
Caged by walls of flesh and bars of bone,
We dream of freedom, but a dream is all it ever is.
The reality of fantasy fulfilled, is too much
For a mere mortal soul to stand. And we run from
Pure freedom as we run from the threat of captivity,
Seldom realizing that the prison of our form
Is stronger than stone, harder than steel.

To dream of gliding on transparent wings up where God
Alone can see, appears to be Paradise, but who would want
To live forever in Paradise? Heaven is where the heart is.
Life within our corrupted walls we choose because we know
What lies there. And what we know is infinitely
Preferable to what we know not.

BUTTERFLY WINGS AND THINGS

WPK

The butterfly lurches
Too long from the meadow
Red hair and violets
Crushed by the street,
Her smile a sinister
Tick in each cheek.

Streets whimper and scream
As pleasure-pain rises
To the air-rifle snap
of high heels on hard tiles.

"My pusher's back there.
I've got my own place.
Two caps and we'll go there.
Quiet and nice.
Drinks and ice.
Twenty dollars, two caps,
And we'll go."

Old men with canes
Tap-tapping the pavement
Like dentists who live by
Discovering decay.

Winos like dandruff
sprawled in dark doorways,
A poncho patterned
In butterfly wings.
The orange of her hair,
The bile of her eyes,
Butterfly wings with
Pin-point dots.
The points of her pupils
Buckwheat in batter.

The orange and the green
A bird flapping at bars.
The wounds in her arms,
Oozing sad blood.

She is butterfly wings
Frayed at the edges
From beating against
Windows she cannot see.

WINO BEGS SPARE CHANGE

WPK

Hunched in a doorway
like a wet bird
as wind whips
at his thin clothes
(the sun is shrill
it is not Wino weather)
Wino extends a hand
dirty as a child's.

The after-five crowd
bustles by, heads bowed
shoulders braced
against the wind.

Leaves and grit
roar around Wino's ankles
assault his sockless feet.
His lips are brown
and his tongue dry
as a fallen leaf. His liver,
inside, small and black
as a dead crow.

MORNING FINDS WINO IN THE WRONG DISTRICT

WPK

With crab-grass face and bleeding eyes
Wino lurches raggedly
into the wrong district
where there are no leaf-filled doorways
full of stale comfort
no sagging flights of stairs
on which to doze:
the sidewalks here are hosed
each morning,
windows scoured.

Wino trembles
as if spiked shoes
were walking down his spine.
He raises his courage to his lips
but the bottle slips
from carrot fingers
cracks like an egg
on the sidewalk.

Wino scuttles into a fresh doorway
slides slowly down the wall.
Inside, jowled faces scowl
until a deep red siren sound
eases their alarm.

WE ARE A SMALL COUNTRY

AK

Remembering Costa Rica

Only the old can afford cars
So there are very few cars,

Still, they run into each other
At almost predictable intervals

More often than tourists lose their
Credit cards, more often than we

Would like. We are a young country.
Trauma is lunch; disaster, dinner.

We like to think nothing happens
Before ten in the morning

That bars on our windows
Will keep the riff-raff out

That only assassins need
Fear our peaceful politicians.

Take justice hostage here
and justice will come out ahead.

We are a small country. We have
time to walk with our children.

SYMPHONIC OVATION

AK

For Marian.

Once, during the second half of the program,
The stringplayers bowed with identical precision.
Each horn was heard to vibrate as one, perfect
Unison. At the final downbeat, the conductor was levitated.
                                And we stopped breathing.

    How long can—this moment—be stretched?

The melody moves into our senses again, unobstructed.
Nothing prevents its washing over us. Every vision,
Synchronous. Beside me, an evening's friend becomes a life partner.
The hall is impossibly reverberant. I hear every song it has known:
                                All I need to pack for heaven.

Friday

The sky is my witness.
—Rodney King

The sky fell long ago.
—W. P. Kinsella

THE KILL

WPK

Little sniffing beasts,
Fish-mouthed, fox-eyed,
Enclose the chosen one.

Bloodflowers bloom
in violent patterns
On the snow.

A shriek circles the valley
Bouncing from mountains
Like a blind bird.

The strong nibble the liver,
The weak wait
On flexed haunches
Inhaling
The salty odor of death.

HOMECOMING

AK

I'd like to pay you another visit—
Maybe unannounced like last time
Or, with a bit more warning.
I'm warming to the sisterhood we share:

Memories not completely remembered.

I took you with me yesterday in fantasy
To the Oregon orchestra master's home.
He conducted us to a room where the silent
songstress, his Aunt Miriam, lay dying.

Do you not completely remember?

You let my hand slip beneath yours, on her
Brown brow, to bless her going and give
Thanks for her being so close
To us at the time of her translation.

Later, in an empty sanctuary, I sang for her.

Do you not remember? "Sometimes
I feel like a motherless child. But,
Not that far from home, tonight, Lord.
Not so very distant from my home."

T.G.I.F. SOLITAIRE

AK

For Elaine

The whales have come again, singing
down the backbone seaspace they move in
haunting me with their invisible profiles

I do not tell them how I yearn to escape these
steely skeletons and mirrored monuments
erected by earthmoving entrepreneurs

I'd be discovered in a secret place
babbling indecent things to heaven about
why they should stop neutering graffiti

STRIPPER

WPK

Pathetic lady
bored
a blue rose
tattooed
on her butt
bumps
out of time
to canned music.

Like peasants
watching
coins counted
rumpled men
too young to be
retired
too wilted to be
working,
gape
lip licking
as forgotten cigarettes
warm yellow fingers.

TAXI

WPK

There's smoke inside my head, mister,
The bar was so hot, and no one was nice to me.
Can you call a person used,
Like a car or a house? That's what
They said about me.

You won't take the long way,
I don't know the city.
I live in a cabin, mister,
Do you believe that?
The bar was so hot, and
The rain is so cool on the window.
I used to be pretty,
Bet you'd never believe that.

Back a long time ago
I remember the rain, mister,
When I was a girl
I used to have curls
Right here, in the middle of my forehead.

I got four boys, mister,
And five girls, only one's gone. . .
I remember the rain.

Published in *ART POOL* from Intermedia Press, 1973.

INHERITANCE

AK

(dripping red) on a
white china platter,
mother's madness
is passed
around the dinner table
with care and contemplation

from his place
at the end,
father calls
"It's for you,"
when the plate
reaches me

I never knew,
now I'm grateful
to have the truth; but the
platter slips as I go
to the kitchen with it.

I stain my fingers
retrieving my inheritance

"Inheritance" appeared in *Poetry Canada Review*, v. 1 no. 4; 1980.

THIS HEAT

AK

If Winter could do one thing, I'd want it
to freeze the thought that something

Better is on the way. We must live in
present tents; nomads, believing

That this heat pushing us past sunset
insists on: the witness of today's sky,

The coming of yet another sabbath,
and our eventual deliverance.

Saturday

JOY: The vigor of an unguarded moment.
WISDOM: The perfection of spontaneity.

THE NORTH SIDE OF MY LIFE
WPK

Dark nasturtiums, deep as summer yolk
That halloween against the snuffy earth,
Musk their way through puce-faced pansy folk
Who stare with scrambled sight, here on the north
Side of my life. Cowbells deceive the ear,
A tinkle here, and here, and here, while thunder
A mastif growl, orders the leaves to bare
Their balmy backs to rain, in rustling wonder.

WINDOW BOXES

WPK

A little bit of sometime, now, they are,
these flowers spindling down the bleak brick wall,
like newly-hatched birds in nests their blossoms
fairly chirp, and seem to ease the grind of bus and car
that cloys the ear and dulls wits like a pall.

Tart little suns that bright grey days, they slip in,
in code, to each dim room around the square,
signs joy persists though life is most unfair:
these window boxes light trite life like prayer.

WEDDING REHEARSAL

AK

Commemorating the spring flowers of the Colorado Desert, 1992-93.

Jimson dons the dress of lily. Slender mitra bears a
violet crown. Chickory, standing in as bride-to-be
is in disguise; as dandelion, in palest yellow, arrives,
the maid of honor. On the marriage bed, verbenia's purple
afghan blushes beneath blankets of golden brittlebush.

Brown-eyed primrose closes weary lids on a cousin's last
remains, dune primrose birdcages, carried off, collectors
say, to display this season's Easter eggs. Now, palo
verde, a green-barked ancient fellow, copies creosote
and friends by adopting yellow. Bottlebrush solos in red.

Mustard's sunny conformity is dread; where nothing
resists, she demands uniformity. Forget-me-not, husband,
comes to his beloved desert lily, white and pregnant
and so proud with her powers, she confesses to him:
I've already conversed with next season's flowers.

PARADE

AK

With a "hat's off" to Noah

Before the overthrow of humanity,
God acceded to requests that an aide leak
The Glorious Latter Day Parade Route and
Fiery Flee Circus Itinerary to CNN. After naming
Seven Chariots prepared for the Last Great Escape
of the First Fourteen Tribes, the plan proceeds:

Then on Monday, gather the burly, the curly
        and the totally unkempt
The paid up, the paid off, the supposedly tax-exempt. . .

On Tuesday, present the clean, the mean
        and the slightly unseemly
The hypocrites and saints who "The Almighty," deem me.
Wednesday, send freaks, especially flame swallowers,
And all those leaders who call themselves followers.

On Thursday, I'll welcome newborns and women,
The anile, the widowers, and those left in prison.
On Friday, let only The Good volunteer
        to join in the train and step to the rear.
On Saturday, athletes, celebrities, and bad-natured
        writers; suvivors, school teachers and tired prize fighters.

Finally, upon the Last Day Of Creation,
        invite anyone left who desires recreation.
We're not letting people slip through the cracks;
        there's even a section for those with bad backs.
No seat is too small and none is too roomy.
We have happiness pills for those feeling gloomy.
So do reconsider, if you said no on Sunday, because
the Last Judgement gates close at12:01, Monday.

SATURDAY MATINEE

WPK

Dismal noon, this faded hour that compresses
The spirit flat against the grimy street
While the lead shroud sky of winter dresses
All the city in blinding black and white.

This life, a long lean queue of rooming houses,
Twilight days, broke-backed cars, and waiting rooms,
And garish signs that bleed out little losses
In green sluiced gutters full of ruin.

Young children tumble puppy-like in line
To view a cartoon show of lambs that run
On popcorn feet, and frolic, frisk and dine,
And draw blue breaths beneath a painted sun.

The children laughed and laughed, gay rainbow sounds,
Clapped their pink hands in new experienced joy,
I cried, not for my past long lost and drowned,
But for their ease the grey years would destroy.

TIME LAPSE

WPK

Pretty as music
she stepped from my past
blown leaf-life from the crowd.
Smiling, I spoke,
moved toward her,
and was young again
until she walked by
blind-eyed
and I remembered
when and where I was.
She looked like a girl
I knew and grew with
and for an instant
I had forgotten that
she too must have
grey hairs
and wear the make-up
of the years.

THE DREAMLAND HALL
WPK

After Vachel Lindsay

Dance a jig-saw dance on a hardwood floor
A strobe light flashing from a metal core
Rolling to the rhythm of the rock band's whack
Float, broken bodies, dancing back to back.
Their throbbing ears pick-up the tom-tom beat
That circles 'round the room on calf-skin feet.
See the brown-faced girls swing on twisted heels,
They sashay smartly as their laughter peals.
Silks and sashes out of dresser drawers
And bargain perfumes from junk-filled stores.
Pale starlight sprayed upon a fly-specked wall,
It's Saturday night at the Dreamland Hall.

Drunk sailors wobble on the upturned floor
As they dance with a squaw last night on shore.
The mean girls bargain to the band's fast clip
Twenty dollars straight, thirty for a strip.
Party dresses, ponchos, and prints all spin
Blue-jeans and jackets and a toothless grin
From old men who slouch and relive their youth
Wine bottle stashed at the side of their booth.
Pay out a dollar and they stamp your hand
A one-way ticket to the Promised Land.
Make it 'til morning, the cruel streets' call:
Forget tomorrow at the Dreamland Hall.

AT REST

AK

And on the seventh day—
no religion was imagined
no hatred nourished; no
movement perceived.

There was a Stillness

no sorrow could penetrate,
no laughter could propel. And, an
affirmation: all manner of thing
shall be well.

Sunday

WPK: Speak to the dead in a common language.
AK: Dance me, O but slower, toward death's stream.

ANOTHER COUNTRY

AK

Recalling Sir Cecil Spring-Rice

Our queen is innured to the call
That earthly kingdoms must fall.
But the prince, rightful heir to
Castles, dismayed; plays out the
Monarchy's death, delayed.

Begun when the Wesleys wouldn't, "Sit
Down, young man," and wait upon the Lord,
But carried the Word themselve to a World
where John's preaching took root, and
Charles' hymns wafted heavenward.

Keeper of God's share of England, Charles
Again, defend your gentlest vow; forgiven
What you did not take. For of the increase
Of Her Bounds, there is only One prepared
To die and rise again today, for Heaven's sake.

NIGHTGOWN

AK

At midnight, sleepless, I stalk the bedrooms of my past —
One in Montana at the center of the house, had
a window onto a back porch. So cold.
Then, that black and white honeymoon suite
("It feels like you're not *living* here!" he said)
in the first house I ever paid-off with
my own money; finally, on the road, I located
the cheapest motel room in all of Michigan — ten dollars.
"Are you the woman the police are looking for?",
the unkempt groundskeeper asked.)

I've opened my eyes to dream in all those places.
Now, here. Now, hear.

ELVIS SURVEYS SOUL
SLAVERY BEFORE THE THIRD MILLENNIUM

AK

He returns; to Sudan. It's Christmas. No reporters, no Marines.

An easy delivery, bone to bone down the long bone tunnel.*

He'll die young, parched on a dry nipple next season, if we

fail to get our collective shit together across this millennium.

"Don't worship my image," the King coos in a foreign tongue.
"Just come to where I Am, and know me in life's magazine:
I'm your devotion, your field of dreams, an angel
needing only what the World needs now.

"Dying skaters, saviours on thin ice,
aid the cause in Somalia, while
in certain quarters their postmortum
becomes a naysayers' projection screen.

"Just get *your* life in gear, and the fear of what might happen
if, will disappear (with Elvis) on the Wind of the Next Millennium.
Last train. Last train for the thousand-year ticket.
Last train to Glory."

*"**Long** bone tunnel," is a quote from poet Shirley Wishart; an adaptation of
Margaret Atwood's "**old** bone tunnel."

THE WILL TO LIVE

AK

In memory of a faithful academician, Judith Sloman

So dance me, O but slower, toward death's stream
I've not resigned from life and pain below.
I'm cradling my tomorrows, nursing a human dream.

If you have fought the fight, then you can deem
Even the struggle, a victory with the foe,
So dance me, O but slower, toward death's stream.

I live one death in public, and it may seem
A tradegy (this cancer), but even as I go
I'm cradling my tomorrows, nursing a human dream.

As a gymnast balanced on her wooden beam,
I test perfection on the status quo,
So dance me, O but slower, toward death's stream.

An autumn sky today is streaked with cream.
Those clouds to me, are signs of hope; they show
I'm cradling my tomorrows, nursing a human a dream.

More skysign wonders now above me teem.
I seem to see more than I need to know.
So dance me, O but slower, toward death's stream
I'm cradling my tomorrows, nursing a human dream.

Published in *Quarry*, vol. 32, no. 1; Winter 1983.

ONE SET OF EYES

AK

For Bill, who is fond of saying,
"I have enough stories for three lifetimes."

Like this child, I am only seven days old—
        or not yet born.
But I've always been expected.
My family carries tomorrow in its genes.

We await the sister
        or perhaps, it is the son—coming
on the scene forty years from this one.
My family carries tomorrow in its genes.

On the boundary with yesterday, a new
        millennium is conducted
To the living. Awaking in these bodies, we
Open one set of eyes at a time.

Tomorrow's stories are coded in our genes.

PUSHING 60

WPK

Bloody borscht stains
Smear my shirtfront
The pocket and above
Is it simple oldfartlyness?
A hole in my spoon?
Bad Luck? Anyone can
Spill soup on their shirt.
That I didn't notice
Until midafternoon, appalls me
Why did no one inform me?

"He's lost his fastball," they whisper
Of the veteran pitcher, but
Never to his face.
"Can't range to the right," they say
Of the old second baseman.
"The aging slugger can't get around
On the fast ball anymore."
In our hearts we all know
Don't need to be told
We're slowing down
Pushing barriers of age
That push back too forcefully

FOR EVERY ANYWOMAN

AK

In celebration of the creation of St. Joan's
Int'l Alliance, Canadian section; March 1979.

I
am
anywoman
I am . . . .
Anywoman Who
anywoman who would
I am anywoman who would invade . . .
who would invade the sanctuary, but not
just the sanctuary, the temple and magisterium, too.

I am Everywoman who will not stop at less
than the very fullest recognition of
her claim to being — *my* claim to
being the token (broken wo-
man) who would dare . . .
dare to claim equality
(in the sight of God
as created) with
 any Everyman;
with every
anyman,
akin
am
I

(Published in THE WITNESS v.63 no.7; July, 1980 and several Catholic newspapers)

INTERACTIVE CONCORDANCE

BIOGRAPHICAL NOTE

Bill (W. P.) Kinsella was born in 1935, in Alberta, to John Matthew & Olive Kinsella. His father, a building contractor, moved to the country during the Depression rather than accept public assistance. Bill lived in isolation the first ten years of his life. In his novel *Box Socials*, Bill reinvents his childhood, "as if something interesting happened to me." Bill met Ann Knight in a writing class at the University of Iowa in 1976, while studying for a Master's degree in creative writing. He is the author of twenty-three books, the father of three daughters, and an enthusiastic reader.

Ann (English) Knight was born in Idaho, in 1943. Her parents were both seminary graduates; her father, a Baptist preacher. Ann joined the Anglican Communion in 1968, and covered the ordination of women debate in the U.S. for readers of *de+liberation*, a quarterly newspaper she founded in 1974, and managed for four years until she married Bill Kinsella, Dec. 30, 1978. With Bill, she co-founded the Calgary Creative Reading Series. She is his bibliographer and archivist, the author of three unpublished novels and three works of privately-printed non-fiction. *Even at this Distance* is her second poetry book; *Rainbow Warehouse*, with W. P. Kinsella (Pottersfield Press, 1989), her first.